VIA CRUCIS

VIA CRUCIS

Meditations on the Stations of the Cross

Ralph Wright, OSB

Paulist Press
New York / Mahwah, NJ

Cover image by Gordana Sermek / Shutterstock.com
Cover design by Sharyn Banks
Book design by Lynn Else

Library of Congress Cataloging-in-Publication Data
Names: Wright, Ralph, 1938– author.
Title: Via crucis : meditations on the Stations of the Cross / Ralph Wright, OSB.
Description: New York : Paulist Press, [2020]
Identifiers: LCCN 2019015263 (print) | LCCN 2019018279 (ebook) | ISBN 9781587688737 (ebook) | ISBN 9780809154777 (pbk. : alk. paper)
Subjects: LCSH: Stations of the Cross—Meditations. | God (Christianity)—Love—Meditations.
Classification: LCC BX2040 (ebook) | LCC BX2040 .W75 2019 (print) | DDC 232.96—dc23
LC record available at https://lccn.loc.gov/2019015263

ISBN 978-0-8091-5477-7 (paperback)
ISBN 978-1-58768-873-7 (e-book)

Published by Paulist Press
997 Macarthur Boulevard
Mahwah, New Jersey 07430
www.paulistpress.com

Printed and bound in the
United States of America

To the happy memory of
MARTIN TIMOTHY WRIGHT
Monk of Ampleforth
April 13, 1942–May 14, 2018
Abbot 1997–2005
Builder of peace and understanding
between Muslims and Christians

CONTENTS

PROLOGUE

A meditation on the Stations of the Cross
articulating the concept
central to our Christian faith
that Jesus's Passion, Death, and Resurrection
reveal the intimate, personal love
that he has for each person he created,
each person he died for.

EXCRUCIATING

Excruciating—
a new word
created for
the new pain
you suffered
when the nails
were pounded
by the soldiers
through your wrists
into the wood
—excruciating—
brought forth
from the cross—
and when
they lifted
the wood
with you hanging
on it
and drove it
into the ground.

Excruciating—
because you created
this speck of dust
—our earth—
only for love
out of love
for me
for each person

in this tiny
corner of the cosmos
which with one word
you created
and hold in being.

Excruciating—
because you are
all power
all knowledge
and all love
so you knew
in eternity
all that would happen
when you uttered
Man
and gave him
the capacity to love
that we call freedom.
And that I
might love you
and live
after this wink
of time
eternally
with you—
you chose the pain
(three hours)
embraced the pain
—excruciating—
and so I am.

STATION I

JESUS CHRIST IS CONDEMNED TO DEATH

Leader: We adore you, O Christ, and we bless you.
Response: *Because by your Holy Cross, you have redeemed the world.*

SCRIPTURE

So Pilate, wishing to satisfy the crowd, released Barabbas for them; and after flogging Jesus, he handed him over to be crucified. (Mark 15:15)

REFLECTION

Jesus, in whom, as St. Paul reminds us, all things were created, is brought before the Roman governor Pontius Pilate for claiming to be "The King of the Jews."

He tells Pilate that his is not a kingdom of this world. Pilate is for releasing him, but a group of scribes and Pharisees, who find his attitude to their hypocrisy more and more intolerable, want him dead.

"We have no king but Caesar!" is their cry.

"And what shall I do with this Jesus?" Pilate asks.

"Crucify him! Crucify him!" is their reply.

Anxious not to cause a riot, Pilate goes along with their demands and hands Jesus over to them to be crucified.

With Imperial Arrogance

God with thorns
braided and fastened
into his scalp
sits
as man
blindfolds and
with imperial arrogance
spits
on his creator. (see John 19:1)

POPE FRANCIS

O Cross of Christ, today we see you in the faces of children, of women and people worn out and fearful, who flee from war and violence and who often find only death and many Pilates who wash their hands.

STATION II

JESUS RECEIVES THE CROSS

Leader: We adore you, O Christ, and we bless you.
Response: *Because by your Holy Cross, you have redeemed the world.*

SCRIPTURE

So they took Jesus; and carrying the cross by himself, he went out to what is called The Place of the Skull, which in Hebrew is called Golgotha. There they crucified him, and with him two others, one on either side, with Jesus between them. (John 19:16–18)

REFLECTION

Unsurprised by Darkness

If God's own Son
had to brink despair,
dying in the darkness
of noonday night,
why should I
know a tranquil passage
from finite groping
to infinite Light,
why am I shocked
by the daily trauma
woven into
the heart of flesh.
The rending anger
perdures from the womb
till the hands are folded.
In the calm of death
see the stars
and ponder the Word
in whom each galaxy
finds its being,
then watch the one
whose humble coming
respects the measure
of our seeing.
For "who can live
with a blazing fire?"

O mercifully, mercifully
hidden God
coming as breeze
coming as bread
coming through the grapes
our feet have trod.

POPE FRANCIS

O Cross of Christ, symbol of divine love and of human injustice, icon of the supreme sacrifice of love and of boundless selfishness even unto madness, instrument of death and the way of resurrection, sign of obedience and emblem of betrayal, the gallows of persecution and the banner of victory.

STATION III

JESUS FALLS THE FIRST TIME

Leader: We adore you, O Christ, and we bless you.
Response: *Because by your Holy Cross, you have redeemed the world.*

SCRIPTURE

After mocking him, they stripped him of the purple cloak and put his own clothes on him. Then they led him out to crucify him. (Mark 15:20)

REFLECTION

Jesus will stumble and fall repeatedly before he reaches the place on Golgotha where the execution will take place. I am reminded of my own failures in the face of evil. Regularly, to cope with my habits of sin, I need to receive the sacrament and pray for the wisdom and humility that will keep me on the path to holiness. I do not realize that I can bear this cross, this temptation, only when I trust in him. I trust in my own strength and so I fall. My first fall is the ordinary confidence I have in my own strength. I know I can keep my balance and I long for this joy, this sensation with such an acute longing that I am sure I will keep my balance.

But I can't. So, I fall. My passion is greater than my love. My lust or ambition or pride or selfishness, unpurified by experience, pushes me on, and I fall. I need to fall to know my weakness and my constant need of the Holy Spirit through whom I may rise to forgiveness and more joy.

O Extravagant

O extravagant
patient God
taking billions
of years to cool
molten light
till life might ripen
into consciousness
competent for your godhead.

O unknown
humble God
choosing to come
without glamour
among the dung
of steaming cattle
and so become
"the eldest of many brothers."

O meticulous
lowly God
choosing to go
without magnificence
nailed between
your brother thieves
proving with unambiguous
deeds
how pure the God
who so conceives!

POPE FRANCIS

Every day we must let Christ transform us and conform us to him; it means striving to live as Christians, endeavoring to follow him in spite of seeing our limitations and weaknesses.

STATION IV

JESUS MEETS HIS MOTHER

Leader: We adore you, O Christ, and we bless you.
Response: *Because by your Holy Cross, you have redeemed the world.*

SCRIPTURE

Meanwhile, standing near the cross of Jesus were his mother, and his mother's sister, Mary the wife of Clopas, and Mary Magdalene. When Jesus saw his mother and the disciple whom he loved standing beside her, he said to his mother, "Woman, here is your son." Then he said to the disciple, "Here is your mother." And from that hour the disciple took her into his own home. (John 19:25–27)

REFLECTION

No words can do justice to this meeting. Mary, who gave birth to him in the stable at Bethlehem, and who, with Joseph, cared for him as he grew to manhood. Mary had so often evoked his miracles—particularly the first at the wedding feast at Cana in Galilee where, prompted by her intervention, he turned water into wine in response to her simple remark: "They have no wine." Now, despite and in part because of all the miracles of healing he had done, she sees him hated by a group of his own people and handed over for execution like a common criminal. The sword of this sorrow went deep into her heart, and we can only imagine how the agony she experienced must have affected her son. When we are tempted not to share the suffering of someone we do not know too well, who is faced with some appalling grief or sadness, let us pray to Jesus for help. He knows how his mother felt at this moment of their meeting. Let us find the courage to reach out to others with comfort and prayer in their time of great need.

Mother and Child

Uncoarsened
by the calluses
of daily decadence,
you feel
the full repertoire
of human wounding
and with eyes

innocent
of all confusion,
you see
there can be
no relief
before the iron
has been driven,
the nerves
have screamed to silence,
and the thing
has been done.

POPE FRANCIS

In my own life, I have so often seen God's merciful countenance, his patience; I have also seen so many people find the courage to enter the wounds of Jesus by saying to him: Lord, I am here, accept my poverty, hide my sin in your wounds, wash it away with your blood. I have always seen that God did just this—he accepted them, consoled them, cleansed them, loved them.

THE CROSS IS LAID UPON SIMON OF CYRENE

Leader: We adore you, O Christ, and we bless you.
Response: *Because by your Holy Cross, you have redeemed the world.*

SCRIPTURE

They compelled a passer-by, who was coming in from the country, to carry his cross; it was Simon of Cyrene, the father of Alexander and Rufus. (Mark 15:21)

REFLECTION

When they find that Jesus is unable to carry the cross, the soldiers grab hold of Simon, a man who has just arrived from Cyrene, and presumably with threats, compel him to carry the cross for Jesus. How often are we compelled to do something that we would rather not do and then later find out that what we did was in fact much more significant than we realized at the time?

Friend

You will be my Simon through the years,
bearing the burden of my loneliness.
From Cyrene,
climbing together
against the gravity of pride,
our calvary,
breaking our toes
against the daily rubble of our falls
and disappointment
you.

Through every joy and grief
passion or despair,
from me
in this hour before eternity,

may God never hide
or in his love
too lastingly or rendingly
divide.

POPE FRANCIS

*O Cross of Christ, today we see you in the faces of con-
secrated women and men—good Samaritans—who
have left everything to bind up, in evangelical silence,
the wounds of poverty and injustice.*

STATION VI

VERONICA WIPES THE FACE OF JESUS

Leader: We adore you, O Christ, and we bless you.
Response: *Because by your Holy Cross, you have redeemed the world.*

SCRIPTURE

Jesus said to him, "Have I been with you all this time, Philip, and you still do not know me? Whoever has seen me has seen the Father. How can you say, 'Show us the Father'?" (John 14:9)

REFLECTION

And now a woman appears; perhaps she was one of the ones mentioned as "watching from a distance." Through the mocking crowd she hurries, despite the looks and comments that come her way. She goes straight to Jesus's side and wipes his face with her handkerchief. This gesture of boldness and compassion moves Jesus deeply. When Veronica returns home, she finds that his face has miraculously been imprinted on the handkerchief. How often have we been moved to help someone whom we barely know but who is in some difficulty or another, but then, through lack of courage or resolution, we have failed to rise to the occasion?

Let Your Face Shine on Us

You came
in Mary's womb
that we might see
your face.

"To see me Philip,
is to see the Father."[1]

We
choose
to terminate
our children

---

1. See John 14:9.

before they might see
even their mother's
face?

And in her
see you,
O Jesus.

POPE FRANCIS

O Cross of Christ, today we see you in simple men and women who live their faith joyfully day in and day out, in filial observance of your commandments.

STATION VII

JESUS FALLS THE SECOND TIME

Leader: We adore you, O Christ, and we bless you.
Response: *Because by your Holy Cross, you have redeemed the world.*

SCRIPTURE

For he said, "Surely they are my people,
     children who will not deal falsely";
and he became their savior
     in all their distress.

It was no messenger or angel
   but his presence that saved them;
in his love and in his pity he redeemed them;
   he lifted them up and carried them all the days
      of old. (Isa 63:8–9)

REFLECTION

The Way Is Hard

The Way is hard,
long, winding, narrow
—sometimes steep—
through woods, valleys,
mountains, deserts
"a lifetime's march"
while the World whispers
to hungry hearts,
"Turn these stones to bread,"
but the Word coming
from the mouth of God
says, "If a child
ask his father
for a loaf of bread,
will he give him a stone?
I tell you this
that my joy
may be in you:
'I and the Father are one.'"

They take up stones
to silence him,
but he passes
through their midst.
Later they come
and he stands still
to let the grain
be harvested,
taken, pounded,
ground to powder,
yeasted, kneaded,
baked, and offered
as food sufficient
for a day's march
—the Way is hard—
come take and eat that your joy too
may be complete.

POPE FRANCIS

*O Cross of Christ, today too we see you in the contrite,
who in the depth of the misery of their sins, are able to
cry out: Lord, remember me in your kingdom!*

STATION VIII

THE WOMEN OF JERUSALEM MOURN OUR LORD

Leader: We adore you, O Christ, and we bless you.
Response: *Because by your Holy Cross, you have redeemed the world.*

SCRIPTURE

There were also women looking on from a distance; among them were Mary Magdalene, and Mary the mother of James the younger and of Joses, and Salome. These used to follow him and provided for him when he was in Galilee; and

there were many other women who had come up
with him to Jerusalem. (Mark 15:40–41)

REFLECTION

And now a group of women—perhaps moved by
Veronica's action, perhaps not; we are not told—together cry
out in lamentation over what is being done to Jesus. Perhaps
some of them or one of their friends has met him or witnessed
one or another of his miracles. He turns toward them and bids
them weep not for him but for their selves and their children.

They did not realize what was happening. The very
Messiah whom they had been longing and praying for had
been rejected by the very people he was coming to save from
the slavery of sin and death. The consequences of this rejec-
tion would lead to terrible sufferings for themselves and for
their children. Within fifty years, their city, Jerusalem, would
be besieged by the Romans and, after its fall, the deaths of
many citizens would follow.

"Pray for yourselves and for your children!"

My Burden Is Light

Come to us, Father, with gifts of new vision,
Come at the end of each night.
Bring to your children who wait in the darkness
The awesome new burden of light.

The burden of seeing that all are given
The dignity shared by your Son;
The knowledge that all should behave as the
    people
In whom your own life has begun.

Come, Holy Spirit, within the day's tedium;
Touch what is drab with delight.
Help us to toil till the cool of the evening
And carry the burden of light—

The burden of being new light to our brothers,
Proclaiming your Word as we live:
The courage to follow the Lord as his servants,
The calm and the grace to forgive.

Come, Lord Jesus, and gaze on your brothers
With gentleness, wisdom, and might.
Help us to shoulder your yoke in the darkness,
Come—for your burden is light.

Be with us always, O Lord, in your mercy
And heal the deep wounds of our pride.
Give us new patience, new joy, and new wonder
And eyes that keep you as their guide.

POPE FRANCIS

*Opening ourselves to God is opening ourselves to oth-
ers. Take a few steps outside ourselves, little steps, but
take them. Little steps, going out of yourselves toward
God and toward others, opening your heart to brother-
hood [and sisterhood], to friendship, and to solidarity.*

JESUS FALLS THE THIRD TIME

Leader: We adore you, O Christ, and we bless you.
Response: *Because by your Holy Cross, you have redeemed the world.*

SCRIPTURE

"Come to me, all you that are weary and are carrying heavy burdens, and I will give you rest. Take my yoke upon you, and learn from me; for I am gentle and humble in heart, and you will find rest for your souls. For my yoke is easy, and my burden is light." (Matt 11:28–30)

REFLECTION

Within a few yards of the place of execution Jesus falls again. This time the soldiers grab hold of him and drag him the few last yards to where the upright beam of the cross is planted. The place, in fact, where the man from Cyrene, a little while previously, had laid down his load.

Infinite Patience

God lets
his Son
be stretched
against
the earth
and nailed
to the wood
of the world.
Behold
the mystery
of infinite
patience
that
God
should create
a being
able
to see
and love

or blindly
hate
then patiently
wait
and not
stop
the entire
show
when an innocent
child
weeps in the
night
or his Son
is stretched
against
the world
and brutally
nailed.

POPE FRANCIS

What has the Cross left in each one of us? You see, it gives us a treasure that no one else can give: the certainty of the faithful love which God has for us. A love so great that it enters into our sin and forgives it, enters into our suffering and gives us the strength to bear it. It is a love that enters into death to conquer it and to save us.

JESUS IS STRIPPED OF HIS GARMENTS

Leader: We adore you, O Christ, and we bless you.
Response: *Because by your Holy Cross, you have redeemed the world.*

SCRIPTURE

And when they came to a place called Golgotha (which means Place of a Skull), they offered him wine to drink, mixed with gall; but when he tasted it, he would not drink it. And when they had crucified him, they divided his clothes among themselves by casting lots; then they sat down there and kept watch over him. (Matt 27:33–36)

REFLECTION

Messiah

Anoint the wounds
of my spirit
with the balm
of forgiveness,
pour the oil
of your calm
on the waters
of my heart,
take the squeal
of frustration
from the wheels
of my passion
that the power
of your tenderness
may smooth
the way I love,
that the tedium
of giving
in the risk
of surrender
and the reaching
out naked

to a world
that must wound
may be kindled
fresh daily
to a blaze
of compassion,
that the grain
may fall gladly
to burst in the ground
—and the harvest abound.

POPE FRANCIS

The Lord calls us to a Gospel lifestyle marked by sobriety, by a refusal to yield to the culture of consumerism. This means being concerned with the essentials and learning to do without all those unneeded extras which hem us in. Let us learn to be detached from possessiveness and from the idolatry of money and lavish spending. Let us put Jesus first.

STATION XI

JESUS IS NAILED TO THE CROSS

Leader: We adore you, O Christ, and we bless you.
Response: *Because by your Holy Cross, you have redeemed the world.*

SCRIPTURE

When they came to the place that is called The Skull, they crucified Jesus there with the criminals, one on his right and one on his left. [[Then Jesus said, "Father, forgive them; for they do not know what they are doing."]] (Luke 23:33–34)

REFLECTION

Your Death Was Ugly as the Cry of Steel

Your death was ugly as the cry of steel
cold and lonely
into the noon night

the terror and the horror
of the nailing
steel on steel on steel on steel on steel

the unmitigated wall
of pain—a barrier that loomed
like an arch across the sky
with all, all, empty of sense

and against the groans and shrieks of agony
from savaged nerves
one word emerged
forgive.

POPE FRANCIS

O Cross of Christ, today too we see you in those persecuted for their faith who, amid their suffering, continue to offer an authentic witness to Jesus and the Gospel.

STATION XII

JESUS DIES UPON THE CROSS

Leader: We adore you, O Christ, and we bless you.
Response: *Because by your Holy Cross, you have redeemed the world.*

SCRIPTURE

From noon on, darkness came over the whole land until three in the afternoon. And about three o'clock Jesus cried with a loud voice, "Eli, Eli, lema sabachthani?" that is, "My God, my God, why have you forsaken me?" When some of the bystanders heard it, they said, "This man is calling for Elijah." At once one of them ran and got a sponge, filled it with sour wine, put it on a stick, and gave it to him to drink. But the others said, "Wait, let us see whether Elijah will come to save him." Then Jesus cried again with a loud voice and breathed his last. (Matt 27:45–50)

REFLECTION

Darkness

There is storm in the desert,
storm in the mountains,
and storm at sea,
but the miracle is
that creation itself
continues to be.

The earth shudders,
rocks are shattered,
houses fall;
lightning nails
the coffin of earth
which darkness palls.

For there on high
nailed to a tree
with man-made steel

are the hands of God
who fashioned Man
on the Potter's wheel.

Above the head
of the woman who bore
the God-man child
a billion stars
of a billion years
are being defiled

For at this hour
and at this place
in the Milky Way,
the life of God
nailed by Man
is draining away.

The wonder is not
that the world quakes
at his final call
but that when he died
the world could bear
to exist at all.

POPE FRANCIS

*The Cross of Christ contains all the love of God; there
we find his immeasurable mercy. This is a love in*

which we can place all our trust, in which we can believe....Let us give ourselves to Jesus, let us give ourselves over to him, because he never disappoints anyone!

STATION XIII

JESUS IS TAKEN DOWN FROM THE CROSS

Leader: We adore you, O Christ, and we bless you.
Response: *Because by your Holy Cross, you have redeemed the world.*

SCRIPTURE

Now when the centurion and those with him, who were keeping watch over Jesus, saw the earthquake and what took place, they were terrified and said, "Truly this man was God's Son!" Many women were also there, looking on from a distance;

they had followed Jesus from Galilee and had provided for him. (Matt 27:54–55)

REFLECTION

How Must It Be for God

How must it be for God,
who hides beneath a Calvary of pain
the massive love he has for each of us,
to know with absolute precision
the mammoth nature of our unconcern,
the cold of our indifference?
Yet he is so afraid of drawing love
for less than kosher motives that he hides
and chooses that his Son should not be seen
except within the guise of one despised;
and that his gentle love should stay unknown
except by those whose almost foolish trust
leads them to tread the path that he once trod
and know, as one ignored and mocked by men,
the wonder of the love beyond the pain.

POPE FRANCIS

*We are called to serve the crucified Jesus in all those
who are marginalized, to touch his sacred flesh in*

those who are disadvantaged, in those who hunger and thirst, in the naked and imprisoned, the sick and unemployed, in those who are persecuted, refugees and migrants. There we find our God; there we touch the Lord.

STATION XIV

JESUS IS LAID IN THE TOMB

Leader: We adore you, O Christ, and we bless you.
Response: *Because by your Holy Cross, you have redeemed the world.*

SCRIPTURE

After these things, Joseph of Arimathea, who was a disciple of Jesus, though a secret one because of his fear of the Jews, asked Pilate to let him take away the body of Jesus. Pilate gave him permission; so he came and removed his body. Nicodemus, who had at first come to Jesus by night, also came, bringing a mixture of myrrh and aloes, weighing about a hundred pounds. They took the body of Jesus and wrapped it with the spices in linen cloths, according to the burial custom of the Jews. Now there was a garden in the place where he was crucified, and in the garden there was a new tomb in which no one had ever been laid. And so, because it was the Jewish day of Preparation, and the tomb was nearby, they laid Jesus there. (John 19:38–42)

REFLECTION

Learn from Me

The grain pounded
to powder
mixed with water
rolled and baked
to become
ordinary bread.

The grapes harvested
trodden
strained
and kept to become
in time
ordinary wine.

The Tree of Agony
the Empty Tomb

breakfast on the shore,
"If you love me,
Simon Peter,
feed my lambs."

Intimacy with God
no ordinary food.

POPE FRANCIS

*O Cross of Christ, teach us that the rising of the sun is
more powerful than the darkness of night.*

STATION XV

JESUS IS RAISED FROM THE DEAD

Leader: We adore you, O Christ, and we bless you.
Response: *Because by your Holy Cross, you have redeemed the world.*

SCRIPTURE

They had been saying to one another, "Who will roll away the stone for us from the entrance to the tomb?" When they looked up, they saw that the stone, which was very large, had already been rolled back. As they entered the tomb, they saw a young man, dressed in a white robe, sitting on the right side; and they were alarmed. But he said to them, "Do not be alarmed; you are looking for Jesus of Nazareth, who was crucified. He has been raised; he is not here. Look, there is the place they laid him." (Mark 16:3–6)

REFLECTION

Sing in Triumph of Our Savior

Sing in triumph of our Savior,
Raise your voices, sing with pride,
Of the gentle one who loves us
And for us was crucified,
Stretched upon the cross in torment,
Healing hatred as he died.

Grieved by Satan's swift deception,
Our creating saving Lord,
Pledged that death should not be final
As the fruit of human fraud,
But that life one day would triumph,
On another tree restored.

Harmony with perfect rhythm
Permeates the balanced plan,
For the Prince of falsehood tumbles—
Meeting truth he cannot stand—

And the weapon that once wounded
Heals within the surgeon's hand.

As the chosen hour of judgement
Struck with lightning's instant flash,
From beyond all time the godhead,
At the Father's timeless wish,
Came into the womb of Mary
And put on our mortal flesh.

Stirring now he lies restricted
In the cattle manger's hold.
Now his mother binds his body
In the bands against the cold.
So the hands of her creator
With her linen she enfolds.

Sing of gall, of nails, of spittle,
Sing of sponge and spear and rod,
How the blows of soldiers opened
Wounds within the heart of God,
And the world of pain found healing,
Bathed within the Savior's blood.

See the noble cross resplendent
Standing tall and without peer.
Where, O Tree, have you a rival
In the leaf or fruit you bear?
Sweet the burden, sweet the ransom,
That through iron your branches bear.

Bend your boughs, O Tree, be gentle,
Bring relief to God's own limbs,
Bow in homage to bring comfort
To the gentle King of kings.
Ease the throne where your creator
Harshly treated calmly reigns.

For of all the woods and forests
You were chosen out to hold
That fair prize that would win harbor
For a drifting, storm-tossed world,
You whose wood has now been purpled,
By the Lamb's own blood enfurled.

May our praises and our wonder
Echo through the heart of light
To the Father who creates us
And the Son whose gentle might
In the Spirit won us freedom
From the grasp of endless night.

POPE FRANCIS

*O Cross of Christ, teach us that the apparent victory
of evil vanishes before the empty tomb, and before
the certainty of the Resurrection and the love of God
which nothing can defeat, obscure or weaken. Amen.*

EPILOGUE

FROM ALL ETERNITY

From all eternity
You chose me
As if to be
Your only spouse.

In time
May I choose you
To be mine.